Saved the Hour

The Rosary Story in Mystery

Anna Burke

VERITAS

First published 2007 by
Veritas Publications
7/8 Lower Abbey Street
Dublin 1
Ireland
Email publications@veritas.ie
Website www.veritas.ie

ISBN 978 1 85390 974 0

10 9 8 7 6 5 4 3 2 1

*A catalogue record for this book is available
from the British Library.*

Designed by Colette Dower
Printed in the Republic of Ireland by Betaprint, Dublin

*Veritas books are printed on paper made from the wood pulp of
managed forests. For every tree felled, at least one tree is planted,
thereby renewing natural resources.*

Contents

Introduction: Entering the Sabbath Space with Mary

Lord, you give us restful hours in your quiet presence. We gather today at the well of inner peace to pray with Mary for she is still, with the holiness of God.

It is evening. The sun has set in the western sky. The Sabbath begins. The sheep have returned from their mountain pasture and the cattle are at rest in the field. The air is silent and the earth is bowed in humble adoration. The rhythm of the week has now ended in the sacred fire of the Sabbath light. We gather at the table to share the Sabbath meal. It is a simple Jewish meal of bread and wine and roast lamb. We pray that the lamb, the sign of liberation, of sacrifice and of God's abiding love, will see us safely to the promised land. As the meal becomes the centre of our unity we are aware that we are part of the great plan of God, that we are immersed in a power greater than us, beyond us. We call down the blessing of the Sabbath on the work already done and on tomorrow's sowing. The lights merge and our hearts beat in gratitude. The strain of troubled emotions subsides and our tired bodies give way to stillness.

At this evening hour God comes to rest with us. It is a time for sharing stories and a time for breaking bread. We recall the mystery of God and we retell the story in the timeless rhythm of the 'Ave Maria'. There is laughter and there is sorrow in our Sabbath space and time is given to remembering.

Mary is our eyewitness as we follow the footprints of the Lord of Lords, the King of Kings. The story is written in her heart and pierced in her soul. As the moon guards this holy hour we know that all is well and that all will be well. We turn to Mary to lead us into the prayer that is deep with longing. We pray with Mary who rested her heart in God's heart.

JOYFUL

My soul magnifies the Lord.
My spirit rejoices in God, my Saviour.
<small>LUKE 1</small>

*The Rosary belongs among the finest and most
praiseworthy traditions of Christian
contemplation. Developed in the West, it is a
typically meditative prayer, corresponding in
some way to the 'prayer of the heart' or 'Jesus
Prayer' which took root in the soil of the
Christian East.* (John Paul II, *Rosarium Virginis
Mariae* 5, 16 October 2002)

The Annunciation

Opening Prayer   We gather today as One Body in Christ. In the love that binds us together we make visible in our time the heart of Jesus. The lighted candle is an expression of the Good News that came from God to the village of Nazareth to burn forever in the human story.

Word of God   The angel said to her, 'Do not be afraid, Mary; God has been generous to you. You will conceive and give birth to a son, and you will name him Jesus. He will be great and will be called the Son of the Most High God.' (Luke 1)

Reflection   With deep thoughts we gaze with wonder into the eyes of God. We are astonished as the star rises in the East. We await the silence of God, to calm our anxieties and to ease our fear. The angel Gabriel heralds our Advent season, and everywhere the flesh is throbbing with mystery. The bare trees are grey with expectation and the rain clouds are moving eastward. Every star in the heavens is splendid with wonder and all creation bends the knee. We pause to wait. We are waiting for a break in the cloud, for a footprint in the sand. We are waiting for a light in the fog, for the comfort of a human voice, for the door to open, for forgiveness to make her way to us. We are waiting.

The Advent road is a highway before us and we scan the distance for the dance of the angels. The old pathways will become highways. The old kings will become shepherds. The fields of corn will become bread from heaven. Sparrows will get special mention and weeds will be given another chance. The old laws will be challenged by love, and people, rejected

6

by human blindness, will be brought to the banquet table. It is a time of new beginnings. The cow will sleep with the bear and the infant child will play in the cobra's den. A river of hope will move through the earth and flowers will bloom in the desert places. The dream of God is being revealed in the son, born of a woman. It is a dream of reconciliation, of loving relationships and of peace. The earth and the heavens will dance on the moon. The young people will see new visions and the old people will dream new dreams. We stand at the edge of dawn.

The First Joyful Mystery

Intercessions   O God, teach us to love.

We pray for our Pope and for Church leaders. May we live our lives by the law of love: *Oh God, …*
We pray for unity among all Christian peoples. May we cross the divide, in love: *Oh God, …*
We pray for people of every race and creed. May the great human thirst for life bind us together more deeply as we make our journey back to God: *Oh God, …*
We pray for people who have distanced themselves from God. May they hear the shepherd calling their names: *Oh God, …*
We pray for ourselves in all our relationships. May the love, the forgiveness and the mercy of God in Jesus be the inspiration of our lives: *Oh God, …*

Concluding Prayer   God of all creation, you make all things for loving. In you there is only life and love, and close to you we grow and become fully alive. Help us to shape a better world as we work together in the body of Christ. We make our prayer in the name of Jesus Christ, who lives with God in the fullness of the Trinity. Amen.

The Visitation

Opening Prayer We gather in prayer today with Mary as she sets out on her mission journey to Elizabeth. We have come to accompany her on the road for we too are the bearers of the Good News. The lighted candle announces the Saviour that we carry in our hearts to the world.

Word of God Mary set out at that time and went as quickly as she could to a town in the hill country of Judah. She went into Zechariah's house and greeted Elizabeth. (Luke 1)

Reflection My morning was busy and I could not answer your call. My evening was short and I could not ask you in. The job was demanding and I could not find time to visit you. The post office was closed and I could not send a card. The car was full and I was unable to carry your bag. My heart was occupied and I had no room for your story. I know that you have tried to make contact with me; you have stopped and you have waited. You have desired a moment of my time, to connect with me and to tell me your good news, but somehow I ran out of time. It would have made a difference to both of us, listening and discovering hope together, but I ran out of time. You wanted to tell me that God had loved you back to life, but I didn't stop to listen to your song:

Someone is coming, a greater person than John the Baptist. It is a time to hope.
Someone is coming, sent by God. It is a time to be amazed.
Someone is coming, linking heaven to earth. It is a time to keep watch.

Someone is coming, carrying a burning light. It is a time to speak up.

Someone is coming, announcing a new law. It is a time to sing.

Someone is coming, a keeper of the promise. It is a time to remember.

Someone is coming, a king to serve the people. It is a time to pray.

Someone is coming, a God in the flesh. It is a time to have time.

The Second Joyful Mystery

Intercessions O Come to us, abide with us, our God, Emmanuel.

God of our Advent waiting, come into our hearts and into our homes; come into our relationships. Child of Bethlehem, give us peace: *O Come to us, …*

God of our Advent longing, come into our anxiety. Child of Bethlehem, give us peace: *O Come to us, …*

God of our Advent darkness, come into the sorrow that fills our hearts. Child of Bethlehem, give us peace: *O Come to us, …*

God of our Advent hope, come into our loneliness. Child of Bethlehem, give us peace: *O Come to us, …*

God of our Advent faith, come into our prayer and worship; come into our loving and giving. Child of Bethlehem, give us peace: *O Come to us, …*

God of our Advent joy, come into the broken pieces of this world, to nations and to hearts at war. Child of Bethlehem, give us peace: *O Come to us, …*

Concluding Prayer Jesus, when you saw where love could take us, you did not cling to heaven but you gave up your home with God to be with us. Your decision to reach out moves us to the very roots of our being. Help us to reach out to others with the news of your love. Amen.

The Birth of Jesus

Opening Prayer   We gather today in God's name with Mary, God's mother, and with the angels who broke the news of Christmas to a waiting world. At the beginning of our prayer time we light the candle of wonder because we have seen the wonder of love in a God who became flesh with his people.

Word of God   The shepherds hurried away to Bethlehem and found Mary and Joseph, and the baby lying in the manger. (Luke 2)

Reflection   Where have I seen that face before? His birth spreads whispers of excitement across the hillside. The people are on their feet; they find their pace in the night. The direction is opened with angel light and the star speeds with wonder to the cattle shed. Where have I seen that face before?

The baby nestles in the breath of the ox at rest, and the mother smiles her sigh of deepest joy. The father guards the breaking news from hungry wolves and the shepherds bow the knee to end the waiting. Where have I seen that face before?

In a village where life is unnoticed he learns the God-plan. In the lake where women wash their clothes and men fish with their nets he is anointed by God and proclaimed as Saviour. In the desert where vipers hiss and demons prey he exposes false promises and marble kingdoms. A lone figure on the landscape of time he walks into our history as the Lamb of God. Where have I seen that face before?

In a world of a billion lights his eyes follow the falling star. In a shelter where poor people find a home, his hand wipes the lonely tear. In a world where power hates company, his heart hears the voiceless cry. In a culture of influence and plenty his footprints lead to a room in Jerusalem. There at the table he leaves enough food for the world. Where have I seen that face before?

The Third Joyful Mystery

Intercessions   Mother of God, pray for us.

In our times of good news and of bad news: *Mother of God, …*
In our times of finding and of losing: *Mother of God, …*
In our times of angel song and of silent nights: *Mother of God, …*
In our times of welcoming and of closing doors: *Mother of God, …*
In our times of seeing and of doubting: *Mother of God, …*
In our times of amazement and of disappointment: *Mother of God, …*
In our times of shepherding and of abandoning: *Mother of God, …*
In our times of wondering and of waiting: *Mother of God, …*
In our times of dying and of being born: *Mother of God, …*

Concluding Prayer   God of our Bethlehem journey, you found Mary in a dark and waiting world and in her eyes you saw the hope of a dawn for all creation. We thank you today for the woman who gave you the flesh of her flesh and who carried the light for the world.

The Presentation of Jesus

Opening Prayer We gather today with Anna and Simeon and with all people who wait in hope to see the face of God. At the beginning of our prayer time we light the candle of hope because the Word is made flesh and we have heard the news.

Word of God The time came for Joseph and Mary to perform the ceremony of purification, as the Law of Moses commanded. So they took the child to Jerusalem to present him to the Lord. (Luke 2)

Reflection The night was still. The moon was keeping watch. Then a soft breeze stirred the desert sand. My heart began to beat again. I saw the dark sky yielding to the dream of God. It was a star of great intensity, like a mirror of gold, holding the universe. I was drawn as if to a magnet, beyond myself, into the sign. I was unable to make the journey to Bethlehem and Anna and myself agreed to keep watch at the Temple gate. We had waited in hope, over a lifetime of days, and on this night we were standing at the dawn of history.

He had been sent by God to redeem the universe story, to fight with fire for the hearts of the people. He had been sent by God to unblock the waterways and to bring bread to famine lands. He had been sent by God to release for poor people their buried treasures. He had been sent by God to make love the option, to call all things into love's keeping and to destroy the enemy of love.

Anna was silent with emotion. I was still with peace. We would meet the King of Kings here at the entrance to the Temple. I knew that he would find us, that our eyes would meet in an instant and that he would recognise the man and woman who waited. I remember taking him in my arms as the winner takes the prize.

In that moment my life was complete; I was holding the Light. Anna spread the news to all who passed by and as the crowd gathered I had a quiet word with Mary and Joseph. Mary seemed to understand what I meant when I spoke about the price of love and how it pierces hearts and souls with the sharpness of a sword.

The Fourth Joyful Mystery

Intercessions   Help me to wait in hope for you.

When the night closes in around me: *Help me …*
When I search for peace: *Help me …*
When I follow the path to nowhere: *Help me …*
When I pray for hope: *Help me …*
When I fall on the rocks: *Help me …*
When I let go to old age: *Help me …*
When my dreams begin to fade: *Help me …*

Concluding Prayer   God of our searching hearts, you kept your promise to bring us back to the Light. With Simeon I take you in my arms and I proclaim to the world that you are the child who will free Israel. May every knee bow to you, O Child of the Rising Sun. Amen.

The Finding of Jesus in the Temple

Opening Prayer As we gather for prayer today, we join the teachers in the Temple to listen deeply to the words of the boy from Nazareth. At the beginning of our prayer time we light the candle of insight, for Christ leads us to the deepest water.

Word of God On the third day they found him in the Temple, sitting with the Jewish teachers, listening to them and asking questions. (Luke 2)

Reflection The village was my first home. I learned the language of the rural community, rich in Hebrew idiom and referenced in the wisdom of the prophets. The people of Nazareth talked in story and the story held their most precious memories. The evening hours around the fire were family times and we sang and danced into the night. You can still find me in family circles where people look out for one another and where love keeps the turf on the fire.

Nazareth was a great place to grow up. Food was plentiful and, when in season, we fed from the berries and grapes and pomegranates. I always enjoyed going to the hills with the shepherds and learning the names of the sheep. The shepherds knew their sheep and they knew the earth and the movement of the clouds and the signs of the sun. They lived out their lives in the rhythm of the seasons, rising with the dawn and going to rest with the sunrise. You can still find me in the soft breeze, in the storm clouds, in the rolling sea, in the snowdrops and in the daisies.

My father and mother, Mary and Joseph, were hardworking people. In my mother's arms I was nourished with a love beyond all telling. Joseph was a carpenter and he taught me the importance of doing things well and of completing the task. Joseph saw the unique possibility in each piece of wood and he often worked at his trade long into the night. You can still find me where people work together, where their work is valued, in conditions that are dignified and fair. It is really not difficult to find me because where you are, I am.

The Fifth Joyful Mystery

Intercessions   Jesus, help us to hear your word.

For all who speak in the name of Jesus: May we live as Jesus lived: *Jesus, …*
For all who hold positions of authority: May we serve as Jesus served: *Jesus, …*
For all who work in the medical and legal professions: May we decide as Jesus decided: *Jesus, …*
For all who control the media: May we influence as Jesus influenced: *Jesus, …*
For all young people in this challenging time: May we hope as Jesus hoped: *Jesus, …*
For all who teach in a spirit of truthful search: May we teach as Jesus taught: *Jesus, …*
For all who serve to bring freedom and comfort: May we heal as Jesus healed: *Jesus, …*

Concluding Prayer   God of our journey, you search for your people on the lakeshore, over mountains and obstacles, beyond boundaries. You gave us Jesus, the light of your face, the abundance of your heart, to lead us to your house. May we hear his teaching and follow the light to journey's end. Amen.

LUMINOUS

The Word was the source of life
and this life brought light to the world.
The light shines in the darkness,
and the darkness has never put it out.
JOHN 1

*Moving on from the infancy and the hidden life
in Nazareth to the public life of Jesus, our
contemplation brings us to those mysteries
which may be called in a special way 'mysteries
of light'. Certainly the whole mystery of Christ
is a mystery of light. He is the 'light of the
world'. (RVM 21)*

The Baptism of Jesus

Opening prayer We gather today on the banks of the Jordan River. Jesus is going down into the water. Before our eyes the Son is immersed in God's plan for the people. We light the candle of Baptism to express our faithfulness to the plan of God.

Word of God Oh, Come to the water you who are thirsty, though you have no money, come! With you I will make an everlasting covenant out of the favours promised to David. (Isaiah 55)

Reflection In the beginning you took the first step. You imagined shapes and colours and light and darkness, and in your breath they came into being. They filled the space with diversity and possibility and in their living together the harmony of giving and receiving began to be heard. This was a new beginning for the empty space and it welcomed the chance to give hospitality to sacred song and to creative movement. God was happy and the relationship deepened. It became so deep that the face of God took shape in a man and in a woman. The love of God was on its course, and the man and the woman lived with God in the garden. They enjoyed the harmony, the interdependence, the dance of the galaxies and the company of the sun, but they desired to control the plan and to act as individuals.

The relationship broke down and God let them go, beyond the garden, into the darkness. Everything suffered. The man and the woman, who were now thinking as individuals, killed the animals and poisoned the grasses and formed relationships with false gods. Jesus, who was with God in the beginning, knew his Father's sorrow and he took on the flesh of the man and the woman to get close to them again. Today, Jesus has come to the Jordan to embrace the saving plan of God. The Father and the Holy Spirit are also there to name and to anoint the one who will reveal on earth the face of God's love. This is God's moment as Jesus takes his place beside us to plead our case. The waters gradually cover his body and he goes down into the world of those who have fallen to the bottom. The people who have followed him to the river are going down into the water to be named with him.

The First Mystery of Light

Intercessions   Praise to God, Father, Son and Holy Spirit.

Blessed be God who creates, redeems and makes holy: *Praise to God, ...*
Blessed be the promise of God, fulfilled in our time: *Praise to God, ...*
Blessed be the timelessness of God, ever ancient, ever new: *Praise to God, ...*
Blessed be Jesus, the well of God's mercy: *Praise to God, ...*
Blessed be Jesus, the face of God's simplicity: *Praise to God, ...*
Blessed be Jesus, the heart of God's love: *Praise to God, ...*
Blessed be the Holy Spirit, the fire of God's passion: *Praise to God, ...*
Blessed be the Holy Spirit, the energy of God's power: *Praise to God, ...*
Blessed be the Holy Spirit, the holiness of God's presence: *Praise to God, ...*

Concluding Prayer   God of our aching thirst, you are the ocean of abundant life and of unknown depths. As we follow Jesus to the Jordan, may we be washed in God's mercy and may the stream of Living Water flow from our hearts all over the earth. Amen.

The Wedding in Cana

Opening Prayer   Our prayer today calls us into the presence of Jesus, the one who makes all things new. The candle is a reminder that the light of Christ opened a new chapter in the universe story. The old wine is finished and the new wine is filling empty hearts.

Word of God   Jesus said to the servants, 'Fill these jars with water'. They filled them to the brim and then he told them, 'Now draw some water out and take it to the man in charge of the feast'. They took him the water, which now had turned into wine, and he tasted it. He did not know where the wine had come from. (John 2)

Reflection   Some things do not match. Round pegs do not fit in square holes. Flat tires hinder the movement of the wheels. False notes destroy the harmony and the sun and the moon cannot shine together. Life is sometimes like a juggling act, and moving forward requires that we get the right thing in the right place at the right time. The message of Jesus and the light that he shone on the world created a new playing field for us. The rules were reduced to one, the One called Love. The referee began recording effort, and struggle and perseverance, rather than counting scores. Even the goal posts changed! Points were now given to the poor in spirit, to the meek and to the merciful ones. Everything was turned upside down. Trophies were presented to those who won and to those who lost, to those who finished and to those who fell.

Someone said that a new heart was possessing the people and that the game was becoming a celebration of life. The people began to put their old wineskins in the museums and heritage centres and they began to make new wine skins for the drink that would quench their thirst and cleanse their vision and bring them life without ending. Mary recognised that a great change was upon the world. She sensed that Jesus would fill empty jars and lead us in a new bridal dance. When the wine ran out at Cana in Gallilee she knew that the people would forevermore drink the wine from the well of God's mercy. Mary calmed the anxious moment by simply asking the waiters to 'do whatever he tells you'.

The Second Mystery of Light

Intercessions   Put a new heart within us, O God.

For all who use authority to oppress other people, we pray: *Put a new heart ...*
For all who control the global economy, we pray: *Put a new heart ...*
For all who wage war and who cause human misery, we pray: *Put a new heart ...*
For all who make family life a place of war and division, we pray: *Put a new heart ...*
For all who will not forgive, we pray: *Put a new heart ...*
For all who have too much and want more, we pray: *Put a new heart ...*
For all who have broken communication with God, we pray: *Put a new heart ...*
For all who have lost hope, we pray: *Put a new heart ...*

Concluding Prayer   God of the heart of Jesus, help us to see with new perception and to hear with new understanding. Cover our pathway with the Light that heals and warms and brings together. May we drink from God's Word the wine of everlasting life. We make our prayer in Jesus' name. Amen.

The Proclamation of the Kingdom and Call to Conversion

Opening Prayer   We gather for prayer today with the faith of one sick man echoing in our hearts. In our brokenness Jesus proclaims a Kingdom where we will be restored to wholeness. The candle calls us to turn our faces to the Light.

Word of God   A man with leprosy came to Jesus and pleaded on his knees: 'If you want to,' he said, 'you can cure me.' Feeling sorry for him, Jesus stretched out his hand and touched him. 'Of course I want to,' he said, 'Be cured!' And the leprosy left him at once and he was cured. (Mark 1:40)

Reflection   I heard a voice coming from the clouds and the rain watered the land in expectation. I heard a whisper coming from the bog heather and the turf turned the swamp to fire. I saw a child lying in a manger and the angels left the heavens to witness the moment. He beckoned to me, the one rejected by the community because I carry in my body the sores of leprosy. There he was, offering to take my sores into his own body. The political correctness of his day would not deter him. He wanted to touch me. This was a new kind of man. He had an inner eye and an ear that heard against the noise and a heart that held on for the extra mile. His eyes drew me into his embrace. 'If you want to … you can …' And he turned and touched me. He touched me. Skin on skin, he touched me. Heart to heart, he touched me. Soul with soul, he touched me. I walked free.

I followed him. I followed the man into Simon's house and I saw the sin turn to tears at his touch. I sat in the boat as the thunderstorm raged and I saw the sea bowing down at his command. I witnessed the attempted murder of the woman whose sin was discovered and I saw her accusers going down on their own sins. I walked in the funeral procession with the widowed woman and her dead son, responded to the breath of the man's heart. I stood on the brow of the hill as the cross was put on view and the rocks split and the sky shook and the graves opened. One soldier said, 'Surely, this was the Son of God'.

The Third Mystery of Light

Intercessions   Lord, may your Kingdom come.

We ask God to guide the Church with wisdom and compassion: *Lord, …*
We ask God to call forth the best in political leaders: *Lord, …*
We ask God to bless Ireland and to renew in us a sense of human dignity: *Lord, …*
We ask God to restore in us a commitment to peace with justice, for all people: *Lord, …*
We ask God to give us a sense of responsibility for the common good: *Lord, …*
We ask God to strengthen our respect for life, from womb to tomb: *Lord, …*
We ask God to forgive us the violence we foster in thought, in word and in deed: *Lord, …*
We ask God to fill our minds with a desire for reconciliation: *Lord, …*
We ask God to welcome the people who have died with hope in the resurrection: *Lord, …*

Concluding Prayer   God of our deepest cry, help us to hear your call to look into your eyes where compassion and forgiveness shine. May we be your heart in the human search for truth and for light. We make our prayer in the name of Jesus. Amen.

The Transfiguration

Opening Prayer   God of all creation, from your ageless being you brought forth time in her centuries, that your people might desire eternal life with you. We who gather today light the candle of time because all time is your time.

Word of God   Jesus took with him Peter and James and his brother John and led them up a high mountain where they could be alone. There in their presence he was transfigured: his face shone like the sun and his clothes became as white as light. (Matthew 17)

Reflection   I arise before dawn to catch the secret of the birth of day. My eyes fill with tears of wonder as the colours merge into shades of new beginnings and the dawn creeps out from the fortress of darkness. I wait, stilled in the holiness of this breathless moment. God is writing the promise into another day. My soul spills over with songs of praise for I have seen the power and the glory. The moon yields her position and the night lets go her fear. It is the communion of heaven and earth and I have seen the mystery.

The world as we know it is passing away. The oceans will be stepping stones and children will run free in every part of the world. The grasses will make spaces for the wild flowers and life will be valued and stories will be heard in every part of the world. The world as we know it is passing away. The storms of destruction will bow down, families will make homes where trust is safe and the child will play in the cobra's den, in every part of the world. The earth will reveal the fullness of her nature and people will dig for the common good in gardens where the worker is valued, where resources are shared and where enough is enough. There will be fair trade and fair influence and fair chance, and justice will be the only human choice, in every part of the world. The ivy leaves will embrace the rose bush and locked doors will become open windows. There will be hospitality and every stranger will be a friend. The desert will bring forth the colours of the rainbow and relationships will be mended in forgiveness, in every part of the world. And there will be mercy. Words will be deep with compassion and the kiss of life will silence the guns. The world as we know it is passing away. God is with us and all will be one again.

The Fourth Mystery of Light

Intercessions We look to God with hope.

We pray for our Pope, for Church leaders and for all of us who form the Body of Christ. May we mark our historic time with the footprints of Christ: *We look …*
We pray for ourselves. May the rhythm of our lives honour the sacredness of time: *We look …*
We pray for justice. May our actions bring hope to economically-poor people: *We look …*
We pray for the empires of wealth where trade is controlled. May the values of caring and sharing take root in human choice and in human hearts: *We look …*
We pray for a renewal of the spiritual sense in our homes and in our parish. May all our plans and dreams lead us to our destiny with God: *We look …*

Concluding Prayer God of our seeking and of our searching, call us forth every day from the things that blur our vision. Give us an awareness of the sacredness of time and lead us gently to that place of abandonment and peace where we meet you face to face. Amen.

The Institution
of the Eucharist

Opening Prayer O God, you are truly present where people live as one. You are the healer of souls and the mender of broken pieces. We are united in your universal call to live in harmony and in peace. The lighted candle calls us into your communion.

Word of God As they were eating he took some bread, and when he had said the blessing he broke it and gave it to them. 'Take it,' he said 'this is my body.' Then he took a cup and when he had returned thanks he gave it to them, and all drank from it, and he said to them, 'This is my blood, the blood of the covenant, which is to be poured out for many'. (Mark 14)

Reflection In the beginning, God saw the possibility of unity in the web of life. The Light and the Darkness would share their mystery and all creation would enjoy together the rhythm of work and Sabbath. A great harmony of giving and receiving was born. The Eucharist of heaven and earth was alive and all creation sang in chorus. The human person with language and with self-conscious awareness brought greater possibility for good and for evil to the web of life and, in time, relationships became fractured and there was breakdown. Darkness spread and the day became as night. The dream of God for unity in the web of life was kept alive by Jesus, the Son of God. He who was with God in the beginning emptied himself and became as we are. In his offering of unconditional love, Jesus restored broken creation to communion with God. Thank you dear God for your love, poured out in Jesus. Thank you for the human mind that thinks noble thoughts and desires communion. Thank you for eucharistic hearts that reach beyond the limits, for the sake of justice and truth and right. Thank you for the splendour of things, for your victory in the mountains, for your mystery in the oceans, for your abundance in the meadows. Thank you for time that gives us long days and quiet nights, happy hours and special moments. Thank you for forgiveness. You lift us up in the heart of Jesus. You offer us communion.

The Fifth Mystery of Light

Intercessions Thanks be to God.

I was able to get up this morning and praise God: *Thanks be …*
I was able to work today and earn a living: *Thanks be …*
I was able to sing today, a song of joy: *Thanks be …*
I was able to speak on the telephone and reassure a friend: *Thanks be …*
I was able to cook, to eat and to enjoy good flavours: *Thanks be …*
I was able to drive the car safely: *Thanks be …*
I was able to feed the birds and to see their appreciation: *Thanks be …*
I was able to read a book and to tell the story: *Thanks be …*
I was able to pray and to spend time with God: *Thanks be …*

Concluding Prayer We thank you God for the wonder of your dream to restore all creation in Jesus. May Eucharist begin with us. May we sing in harmony with the earth community, that through our words and actions the world may know that you are One. Amen.

SORROWFUL

… And sorrow like a sharp sword
shall break your heart.
Luke 2

*Never as in the Rosary do the life of Jesus and
that of Mary appear so deeply joined. Mary lives
only in Christ and for Christ. (RVM 15)*

The Agony in the Garden

Opening Prayer We are challenged in our prayer today by the reality of the grinding poverty that oppresses millions of people. We unite our hearts with the agony of people who have no bread. The candle flame reminds us that our love can defeat the darkness.

Word of God On the earth you have had a life of comfort and luxury; in the time of slaughter you went on eating to your heart's content. It was you who condemned the innocent and killed them; they offered you no resistance. (James 5)

Reflection There are no level playing fields in life. The advantage is with those who are strong and swift, and society bestows her graces on the rich and on the famous. Influence and power are most frequently bought and money largely determines how the victory is won. There is fair trade for the few and there is no trade for the many. In the scramble for today's bread, bodies get sold and children become slave workers. But the earth is growing silent. She is withdrawing from the violence of greed and she weeps for her hungry children whose right to live has been withdrawn by those who devour the fat and drink the cream and throw away the remains.

O Gethsemane! A child cowers in the darkness outside my window. Her slouched body seeks shelter against the oak tree but the tree is bare in her wintertime.
O Gethsemane! A woman carries her children to the safety of the night shelter. She stops for breath against the streetlight but the light flickers and fades.

O Gethsemane! A man stretches out on the park bench. He rests his head on yesterday's newspaper and reaches for another drink to bring on the night, but the can is empty.

O Gethsemane! The children stumble from the bus, poisoned with alcohol. They walk on broken bottles and fall in shallow gutters but there is no one to lead them home.

O Gethsemane! The birds search for berries but the bushes are bare. The peoples' dream is washed away in the agony of the ocean wave.

O Gethsemane! In the shade of your olive tree I see a young man. His heart is bleeding with the sorrow of his people.

The First Sorrowful Mystery

Intercessions   Lord, help us to hear the cry of those in need.

You called us into your family to be a people of compassion: *Lord, …*
You called us into your plan to be a people of hope: *Lord, …*
You called us into your light to be a people of courage: *Lord, …*
You called us into your mission to be a people of justice: *Lord, …*
You called us into your heart to be a people of love: *Lord, …*
You called us into your life to be a people of holiness: *Lord, …*
You called us into your house to be a people of generosity: *Lord, …*
You called us into your body to be a people of communion: *Lord, …*

Concluding Prayer   O God, renew in us today your spirit of justice and mercy. Awaken in us a commitment to challenge the structures that promote and sustain poverty and oppression. May our sense of justice become an action for justice. We make our prayer in the name of Jesus, the Just One of God. Amen.

The Scourging at the Pillar

Opening Prayer   Today, we begin our prayer aware that our world is unequal and unfair. We pray with our sisters and brothers who pay the price of greed. The candle reminds us that some people recognise the cry of the innocent and give all they have to give.

Word of God   So Pilate, anxious to placate the crowd, released Barabbas for them and, having ordered Jesus to be scourged, handed him over to be crucified. (Mark 15)

Reflection   I was whipped for the sins of the guilty. The blows rained down until my skin fell apart, but violence has no power over me. Violence has no power over love. It is the tool of weak people, of people who live in emptiness. They could not make space for a King without a throne. They would not be lifted up by a man without an army so they did what defeated people do; they used physical force against me and they called it a victory.

As my body broke in pieces I cast my net to the ocean bed and with my blood I marked a highway in the deep, a single trail of crimson light crossing over, reaching under, giving a foothold to those who have been beaten to the dust. I know the ones who are left behind, whipped to silence by verbal and emotional abuse. As the lashes sank into my flesh I spoke their names for them and I held on for them. My cry was their terror; my scream was their misery. I was beaten with the homeless children, with the voiceless women, with the innocent prisoners. I became the prey of greed and power, something to be stripped to the bone, for I was an uncomfortable presence before the glory of Rome.

When they finally cut me down, the pillar was stained with shame. Nothing had been won; I was still loving them. They slunk away into the shadows, the soldiers with their achievement. They knew that the sword had let them down. Pilate also saw his mistake, but weakness cannot admit defeat and they led me to the cross.

The Second Sorrowful Mystery

Intercessions   May we be generous in giving.

We pray for the Church, the Body of Christ on earth, that she may give witness to the generosity of God: *May we …*
We pray for people in the caring professions, that they may find joy in giving: *May we …*
We pray for people with great economic wealth, that they may give back what they owe: *May we …*
We pray for parents and guardians of young people, that they may teach the values of sharing and caring: *May we …*
We pray for young people, that their dreams may include a responsibility for people who are oppressed by poverty: *May we …*
We pray for ourselves, that our hearts may be big in giving and in forgiving: *May we …*

Concluding Prayer   O God, you are our faithful friend. You entered the empty space of our lives and you lit an eternal flame. Help us in our time to carry the light to the ends of the earth and especially into the lands darkened by famine, disease and fear. May our giving be without cost. We make our prayer in Jesus' name. Amen.

The Crowning
with Thorns

Opening Prayer Christ is our rock. We gather today in the safety of his strong arms. The lighted candle reminds us that the presence of Christ in our time is a light that is not intimidated by darkness. This light will not be defeated.

Word of God I shall be very happy to make my weaknesses my special boast so that the power of Christ may stay over me, and that is why I am quite content with my weaknesses and with insults, hardships, persecutions and the agonies I go through for Christ's sake. For it is when I am weak that I am strong. (2 Corinthians 12)

Reflection When the darkness gathered in my life, I learned to wait patiently for the light. When thorns pierced my flesh, I learned to endure the sharp word and the harsh judgement. When the weight of broken relationships brought me to the ground, I learned how other people live and how the heart does go on. When there was no one left to understand me and my spirit numbed within me, I learned about giving others a chance. When my best efforts failed, you waited for me and I learned about starting again. When I made destructive decisions and lost myself in a fog of abusive behaviour, you raised me up and I learned how steadfast love can be. When I gave up in weakness, you showed me your crown of thorns and I learned about inner strength.

Every moment of my life has been shaded in light and darkness, sometimes merging, sometimes balancing, always teaching. In every stumble I found choices; in every fall I faced decisions. In every strength I rejoiced and in every strength I found limitation. There was in every experience someone guiding, someone supporting, someone waiting for me. A hand held mine and led me through the maze. A heart held mine at the breaking point and I touched the face of Mercy. The crown of thorns opened my soul and the searing pain gave me an awareness of the wonder of the human spirit. My weakness has become my strength. I set my compass to deeper water, to places of wisdom and harmony where the spirit triumphs and where love goes on. When I am weak, then I am strong.

The Third Sorrowful Mystery

Intercessions   Christ, be my strength.

When my faith flickers and starts to die: *Christ, …*
When my love weakens and gives way to apathy: *Christ, …*
When my efforts fail and my confidence dies: *Christ, …*
When my love is ejected and I feel alone: *Christ, …*
When my family separates and I have no answer: *Christ, …*
When my job closes down and I am in debt: *Christ, …*
When my words are not heard and I am silenced: *Christ, …*
When my cry for help is ignored and my tears fall: *Christ, …*
When my loss is great and my body shuts down: *Christ, …*

Concluding Prayer   O God of our nights and of our days, you are the rock of safety in our night of storms. Save us in our weakness. Show us your face in the shadows and lead us into the light. We make our prayer in the name of Jesus, our forever friend. Amen.

The Carrying of the Cross

Opening Prayer   O God, our hearts are full of gratitude because your heart is rich in mercy. You carried us on your shoulder and you absorbed the weight of our sins. The light of the candle reminds us that you have set us free.

Word of God   Then they took charge of Jesus, and carrying his own cross he went out of the city to the place of the skull or, as it is called in Hebrew, Golgotha, where they crucified him with two others. (John 19)

Reflection   I strained forward on that last mile, without strength, my mind shut down with pain, my body cold with sorrow, but I was loving you on that last mile.

I held on for that last climb. My blood was forming a pool of teardrops; my flesh was thirsting for the hearts I had not reached, but I was loving you on that last climb.

I let them do as they wished in that last hour, without remembering it against them. The courage of Simon and Veronica kept me going, and I was loving you in that last hour.

I kept a word of forgiveness for that last breath, without any hope of being heard against the noise of those who drown the evidence. One of the soldiers looked at me as if to say 'Thank you', and I was loving you in that last breath.

I looked to the men beside me in that last call, without condemnation, wanting to draw them to my heart. One man looked me in the eye; he wanted to be with me. I rescued him and the one who looked away, for I was loving you in that last call.

I gave you my mother in that last moment, without counting the cost, to hold you together and to keep the heart in your new beginning. She, who survived this final chapter, would plead your cause in heaven, for I was loving you in that last act.

I heard the thunder roar and the tombs splitting the rocks. The spirits of the dead appeared on the hillside and my cross of shame shook with the strength of God's power. A soldier touched my feet and the last words I heard were, 'Surely this man was the Son of God'. I died then, but I was loving you in that last victory.

The Fourth Sorrowful Mystery

Intercessions   We place our trust in you, O God.

For peace on the earth and in every human heart, we pray: *We place …*
For hope in times of sorrow and loss, we pray: *We place …*
For faith in times of failure and rejection, we pray: *We place …*
For perseverance in times of doubt and fatigue, we pray: *We place …*
For faithfulness in times of betrayal and conflict, we pray: *We place …*
For forgiveness in times of hurt and misunderstanding, we pray: *We place …*
For courage in times of weakness and fear, we pray: *We place …*
For calmness in times of anxiety and uncertainty, we pray: *We place …*
For love in times of coldness and hostility, we pray: *We place …*

Concluding Prayer   God of great mercy, through your son, Jesus Christ, you revealed your heart to a waiting world. We see in Jesus a love beyond all telling and in his name we thank you for your love and your forgiveness. Amen.

The Crucifixion

Opening Prayer   Into your hands, O God, we place our lives today. As we gather for prayer we come in a spirit of service, for we stand at the foot of the cross where the servant king gave his life. With lighted candle we keep watch at this sacred hour.

Word of God   When they reached the place called the Skull, they crucified him there and the two criminals also, one on the right, the other on the left. (Luke 23)

Reflection   I am among you as one who serves. I took your shape and form, and in the flesh that limits and fades and dies I entered into your human experience, to bring you back, to guard your destiny. In the cloth of a shepherd I walked through the hills and valleys, searching every crevice and rock. I uncovered the undergrowth and I took on the cliff's bare edge to find the stray ones, to rescue the lost ones. The boundary lines moved back to let me pass, and in the homes of ancient foes, where doors were sealed and fences secured, I sat at table and joined the feast. Day by day, I watched for my prodigal child. The candle in my window was the sign that I was awake and waiting for your return.

I bathed the festered sores of tired feet and eased the wound of heart and soul. The years of desert dryness were brought to life in a spring of living water. It poured out from my side and opened the pores of the dying earth and the people came with longing to be washed and to be renewed. I poured out my love until it became the blood of life for the faithful ones and for the unfaithful ones. It filled broken vessels and ended the power line. When they pierced my heart the songbirds cried but the water became the river linking the people to the ocean. The earth bowed down in her restoration hour and all creation stirred with new beginnings. With my arms outstretched I linked the compass points of the cosmic map. The grip of fear loosened in the heat of the sun, for the Promise of God was fulfilled on the wood of the tree.

The Fifth Sorrowful Mystery

Intercessions   Thank you God for your great love.

You give us wise and holy leaders who speak with the love of Jesus: *Thank you God ...*
You give us brave and prophetic people who influence world order: *Thank you God ...*
You give us loving and caring parents who teach us to pray: *Thank you God ...*
You give us prosperity and good things for our enjoyment: *Thank you God ...*
You give us generous and responsible people who work for the common good: *Thank you God ...*
You give us gifts of body and mind to create beautiful things: *Thank you God ...*
You give us kind and gentle people who care for those in pain: *Thank you God ...*
You give us Christian communities to worship and to celebrate life: *Thank you God ...*
You give us Mother Earth to nourish us and to teach us: *Thank you God ...*

Concluding Prayer   O Healer of nations, you sent Jesus to restore all creation and to return it to you as a holy offering. He lives on with us as healer and teacher and friend. We praise and we thank you, God, for the servant King who became as we are, that we might become as he is. May our love also endure from age to age. Amen.

GLORIOUS

Why are you looking among the dead for one who is alive?
He is not here; he has been raised.

LUKE 24

*The Rosary is both meditation and supplication.
Insistent prayer to the Mother of God is based
on confidence that her maternal intercession can
obtain all things from the heart of her Son.
(RVM 16)*

The Resurrection

Opening Prayer This is the day! The joy in our hearts is spilling over, for this is the day of victory. As we begin our prayer we light a flame of life and our cry goes out to all the world, 'Alleluia'.

Word of God 'Do not be afraid,' he said. 'I know you are looking for Jesus of Nazareth, who was crucified. He is not here – he has been raised!' (Mark 16:6)

Reflection These were uncertain days, and we sought the shadows of the trees as we hurried to the tomb. We were silent with tension at this pre-dawn hour, for we had stood firmly to the death beside the one who had challenged the power of Rome. We knew, however, that women had a reasonable chance of safe passage since the Roman officials were familiar with our burial rights.

On the morning of that third day we moved as one, elbows touching, footsteps in rhythm, as if to reassure the other. The only obstacle would be the stone, a large slab of mountain rock, securing the body against possible theft. We feared the worst, that this early morning ritual was indeed the end, but our thoughts remained unspoken.

There had been other obstacles along the way and following the call of the man from Galilee it had been an exciting but dangerous adventure. He had dared to invite women to his table and we had dared to love him openly. He had eagerly sought out our wisdom and we had inspired him with our mercy.

I remembered how Jesus had moved away some of life's great stumbling blocks. He had unblocked eyes and ears and hearts and souls. The storms bowed down before him, the sinners stood up beside him and, at the sound of his voice, the dead began to live again. With the strength of these memories we faced the great stone that sought to bury our dream.

The stone was pulled back and the tomb was open! Instead of relief I felt panic. This was a serious situation. The very evidence of his death was gone. My only clear memory of the next hour is that I was running and Peter was running and the other disciples were running. We could cope with death; we could not cope with chaos. We were scattered and torn with disbelief. I turned to the gardener and begged him for any information that might give direction to the search. His calmness gave me back my breath, and when he spoke my name I cried with love. He asked me to tell the others that the final stone had been rolled back.

I remember speaking the words. They came from my mouth, first in a whisper washed with tears, then in a woman's cry, breaking with joy, sighing with fullness. As I sank to the ground and kissed the soil where he had lain I knew that death was defeated for ever. At the dawning of the day, I called out to Peter, 'He is risen'.

The First Glorious Mystery

Intercessions   My soul praises God.

Jesus is Risen! With all creation we rejoice before the empty tomb: *My soul …*
Jesus is Risen! With Mary Magdalene we proclaim to the world that this is the day of hope, the day of victory: *My soul …*
Jesus is Risen! With Peter and the Apostles we run with joy to tell the Good News: *My soul …*
Jesus is Risen! With the whole Christian Church we pray that our faith in this moment may be strong and sure: *My soul …*
Jesus is Risen! With all who live entombed in darkness we pray that life may return to our bodies: *My soul …*
Jesus is Risen! With all who are sick we pray for the power of the resurrection in our minds and in our hearts: *My soul …*
Jesus is Risen! With all who mourn the dead we pray that the victory of Jesus over death will give us comfort and hope: *My soul …*

Concluding Prayer   God of the risen Jesus, you are the source of life. Today, as we look deeply into the heavens we open our arms to the rising sun. We praise you, God, for the triumph of Jesus. We thank you for the love of Jesus. With the whole community of believers we sing the song of life without ending. Jesus is risen! Alleluia! Amen.

The Ascension

Opening Prayer It is time to say goodbye. As we gather in prayer today we are aware that a chapter is closing and that we will open the new chapter. The light of the candle assures us that presence lives beyond the grave and in his going from us Jesus lives on for ever in hearts that love and remember.

Word of God After the Lord Jesus had talked with them, he was taken up to heaven and sat at the right side of God. (Mark 16:19)

Reflection The time has come and I must leave you, for it was the plan that I would return home to my God and to your God. I am going up now, beyond the clouds, into another time where life is deeper and where love is all.

I am going to prepare a place for you and I will long for your return until we meet again. You are much more than a memory: you are family and you are mine. Before time, in time and beyond time your names are written. We are linked in a blood bond as God promised Abraham. I am going up now and you will not see me but you will find me in the Bread and that will be our communion. I am going over the horizon where rivers flow into the sea of light, where eyes see richer colours and ears hear angel songs. I will keep a place for you so that wherever I am you will be there too. In this in-between time, as you wait for my return, go out to all the world and tell the Good News.

The Second Glorious Mystery

Intercessions   Lord, come back for us.

Lord, on this day you ascended into heaven. Your victory is complete. We ask you to remember your Church and to stay with us for ever. We pray: *Lord, ...*

Lord, on this day your work on earth is complete and you ask us to continue what you started and to be your voice from age to age. When our work on earth is over, we pray: *Lord, ...*

Lord, on this day you complete the bridge between heaven and earth. Help us to remain strong in faith and hope as we await our crossing over. We pray: *Lord, ...*

Lord, on this day you return to your God and to our God. May the light of your love burn in our hearts always. We pray: *Lord, ...*

Lord, your Ascension fixes our eyes on our eternal destiny. When life is difficult and uncertain help us to remember that you promised to come back for us. We pray: *Lord, ...*

Lord, bring all who have died with you beyond the clouds, and may we all be reunited one day in the place we call home. We pray: *Lord, ...*

Concluding Prayer   God of beginnings and of endings, as we witness the return of Jesus to his home in you, we know that we are now the stewards of the story. May we be the faithful witnesses to a love that destroyed death, and in that love may we be taken one day beyond the clouds. We make our prayer in the name of Jesus. Amen.

The Descent of the Holy Spirit

Opening Prayer   Come Holy Spirit. Lead us into God's presence. Teach us how to pray. As we light this candle we pray that your energy may flow through us and from us.

Word of God   They were all filled with the Holy Spirit and began to speak foreign languages, as the spirit gave them the gift of speech. (Acts 2)

Reflection   Near Jerusalem, in a safe house, the people whispered thoughts of fear. They talked to keep the silence out. Their support base had crumbled and their questions were now leaning to doubt. The men paced the floor and the women cooked the bread. In a voice that broke with uncertainty, Peter insisted that something would happen soon. He seemed to base his hope on the friendship he had shared with Jesus rather than on any specific teaching. Mary Magdalene was unusually silent during these days. Her grief was great but her conviction never wavered. She went even further than Peter and said that something never heard before was going to happen. She knew that it had already happened in her own soul. Mary, the mother of Jesus, encouraged everyone to eat and to rest. She poured the wine and talked about Jesus as a little boy. When she recalled Cana, she said that she felt it had something to do with the thirst in our hearts for God's love.

It was the evening of the ninth day and the little group was already fatigued in the confines of uncertainty. It was Andrew who alerted the others to a rumbling sound in the roof. They listened and their worst fears were magnified. They were under attack! The rumble turned to the sound of wind. It was strong but nothing stirred. The wind gathered strength and it blew over them and through them. It seemed to anoint them and to embrace them. No words were spoken as, one by one, the men and women broke into song. They sang of Moses and of freedom; they sang of Israel and of the Promised Land. The wind turned to fire. They were being washed in a sea of flames. There was laughter and tears and as the fire burned their fear to ashes, Peter pushed open the locked door and ran into the street.

The Third Glorious Mystery

Intercessions   Veni Sancte Spiritus.

Spirit of the Living God, give us Wisdom, to refer everything to God's plan: *Veni …*
Spirit of the Living God, give us Understanding, to read the signs of the times: *Veni …*
Spirit of the Living God, give us Right Judgement, to influence our time with goodness: *Veni …*
Spirit of the Living God, give us Courage, to defend what is true: *Veni …*
Spirit of the Living God, give us Knowledge, to desire to see God: *Veni …*
Spirit of the Living God, give us Wonder, to be amazed at the Love of God: *Veni …*

Concluding Prayer

Spirit of God's energy, touch us with the power of God.
Spirit of God's silence, lead us into the depths of God.
Spirit of God's peace, fill us with the stillness of God.
Spirit of God's light, open to us the wonder of God.
Spirit of God's courage, strengthen in us the faithfulness of God.
Spirit of God's healing, awaken in us the desire of God.
Spirit of God's love, hold us in the heart of God.

The Assumption of Mary

Opening Prayer Jesus, the promise of your return in glory helps us to go on waiting. We believe that the heavens will open again and the song of angels will fill the countryside and we shall see God. The lighted candle directs our eyes to the vision of your glory.

Word of God The Son of Man will appear coming in the clouds with great power and glory. He will send the angels out to the four corners of the earth to gather God's chosen people from one end of the world to the other. (Mark 13)

Reflection In the beginning, God made a promise to the people he had chosen. It was a promise that God loved us and that we would inherit the Promised Land. The people on earth agreed the covenant with heaven and a timeless partnership was born. The relationship was expressed in love's ageless dialect and translated into Greek, Hebrew and Latin. It was written in stone and it was fulfilled in flesh. The promise was the Word and the Word became a human person, having lived with God from the beginning. He opened the vault of heaven and took the covenant to the limits of love. The script was rewritten and the new covenant was signed in blood. This was love's deepest breath from the mouth of the unseen God. The unimagined was now possible as Jesus walked the earth and sat at our tables and joined in our feasts. His words moved stubborn hearts and his touch restored lost sight. His command silenced corruption and storms and his forgiveness raised lives from frozen spaces. The bond was sealed with years of love and the captive ones walked free. The Lamb died for the sheep in the moment of love's victory. The promise had stood, rock solid, unshakable. He will return one day to finish the dream that God had in the beginning. The promise said so! He came back for Mary.

The Fourth Glorious Mystery

Intercessions My soul give thanks to God.

You created every part of me: *My soul ...*
You put me together in my mother's womb: *My soul ...*
You made a covenant with Israel and called her your own: *My soul ...*
You pursue us with an everlasting love: *My soul ...*
You wait for us and you guide us; you forgive us and you take us back: *My soul ...*
You reveal your heart in the person of Jesus: *My soul ...*
You sent your Spirit to lead us in wisdom and in understanding: *My soul ...*
You promised to return for us when Jesus comes in glory: *My soul ...*
You are God without beginning or ending: *My soul ...*

Concluding Prayer God of the Promise, the heavens and the earth speak to us of your abiding presence in all creation. Your fire and your energy fill every shape and every colour. Thank you for the wonder of your faithfulness. May we be loving partners in the holy covenant. We make our prayers in the name of Jesus, who gave everything he had for love of us. Amen.

The Coronation of Mary

Opening Prayer We gather in joy with Mary, for she is now Queen of Heaven. May our faith be real and may it lead us one day into the heavenly chorus. With this lighted candle we express our desire to live in God's house where Mary is Queen.

Word of God Now a great sign appeared in heaven: a woman, adorned with the sun, standing on the moon, and with the twelve stars on her head for a crown. (Revelation 12)

Reflection I am the vine and you are attached to me. Your faith is the sap of life from me to you. You grow out from me, an extension of my service. With you and through you my roots spread out through all the earth. You discover new horizons for me and together we weave a river of life through the land. I am the vine and in me there is only life. Everything that comes out of me is a living thing. Where I cannot take root there is nothing. You are the branches, spreading out from the source, bringing the genetic material of life and of love to all the regions of the vineyard. You are the shelter of my arms; you are the relief of human thirst. You welcome and you nurture; you refresh and you restore in my name.

At harvest time I yield the grapes for the new wine, to fill your table, to secure your waiting time. You are the people of the harvest, reaping what you have sown, drinking from the cup that overflows with life. I am the vine and you are the branches. You are attached to me as the branch is attached to the tree. We share the nerve centre where faith and love embrace, and from the fire we weave the Light through the

50

vein system, opening paths, giving a chance, revealing hope. I hold you as a son holds the mother he loves and I watch with you as God protects the one he loves. We are faces in the crowd, watching out for those who have run out of options.

The Fifth Glorious Mystery

Intercessions   Queen of Heaven, pray for us.

The Church is a broken body and the people walk away: *Queen of Heaven, …*
The voice of God is drowned out in the family conversation: *Queen of Heaven, …*
The values of justice and forgiveness are increasingly unpopular: *Queen of Heaven, …*
The defence of life is frequently rejected: *Queen of Heaven, …*
The reverence for the holiness of the body is mocked: *Queen of Heaven, …*
The care for all creation is seriously frustrated: *Queen of Heaven, …*
The expectation that the good things of life would be shared is ignored: *Queen of Heaven, …*
The longing for your faithful love is often drowned out: *Queen of Heaven, …*
The promise of eternal life is constantly devalued: *Queen of Heaven, …*

Concluding Prayer   God of our hunger and thirst, fill us with the love that filled the heart of Mary. Help us to walk beside you and to follow you with our lives. Mary, Queen of Heaven and of Earth, pray for us. We make our prayer in Jesus' name. Amen.

LENTEN

Standing close to Jesus' cross were his mother,
his mother's sister, Mary, the wife of Clopas
and Mary Magdalene.
JOHN 19

*The Rosary does indeed 'mark the rhythm of
human life', bringing it into harmony with the
'rhythm' of God's own life, in the joyful
communion of the Holy Trinity, our life's
destiny and deepest longing. (RVM 25)*

Jesus is Afraid

Opening Prayer   We gather with you today, O Light of the deepening shadows. From the beginning, your voice has penetrated the emptiness of every form and space and all things have responded to your authority. Today you are alone with the fear of your agony and death. We light this candle to keep you company in your darkest hour.

Word of God   'Father,' he said, 'if you will, take this cup of suffering away from me. Not my will, however, but your will be done.' An angel from heaven appeared to him and strengthened him. (Luke 22)

Reflection   The garden is silent tonight. A strange stillness has descended and I see storm clouds gathering in the East. I feel very alone and I am broken and afraid before an unknown darkness. But I must face this hour for the sake of the ones I love.

The Lord is my shepherd; he will travel with me into the pain. Over the miles of my journey I will find pasture for my hunger and mountain streams will ease my thirst. After the night the sun will rise on my meadows and she will send me warm breezes to bathe my open wounds.

The Lord is my shepherd; I will not fear the swamps and bog holes. The rocks will be my stepping stones, connecting me to bridges, linking me to possibilities. The sharp edges will give me understanding and the slippery slope will give me a compassionate heart.

The Lord is my shepherd; I will rest from anxiety and stress. In every desert I will find a cactus plant and on every cliff edge I will find a hand in mine. The waves of darkness will never blur my dream and I shall be put together in the dawn light.

The Lord is my shepherd; he waits for me at every crossroads. His eyes follow my footsteps and his love releases the briars that ensnare my body. As I seek the destiny of my desire I shall not be choked by weeds. God will be there to find me and to carry me home. When I sleep he is awake. These eyes of love never leave me. God is my shepherd; I have no fear in the garden of silence.

The First Lenten Mystery

Intercessions   Stay here and watch with me.

Lord, I am afraid of tomorrow's news: *Stay here ...*
Lord, I am walking in shadows: *Stay here ...*
Lord, I am waiting in darkness: *Stay here ...*
Lord, I am expecting death: *Stay here ...*
Lord, I am frozen in silence: *Stay here ...*
Lord, I am standing at the edge: *Stay here ...*
Lord, I am calling out to you: *Stay here ...*

Concluding Prayer   Spirit of the Living God, we ask you to be our strength as we struggle with the dark places in our hearts. Stay with us, O Holy Spirit; hold us when we fall and give us courage for the longest mile. We make our prayer in Jesus' name. Amen.

Jesus is Betrayed

Opening Prayer   God of the Faithful Promise, we desire to be your faithful people. May our prayer today tell of our love for you. You are the destiny of life and we long to return to the place where you live. The candle speaks to us of your warm and faithful love.

Word of God   Then Judas Iscariot, one of the twelve disciples, went off to the chief priests in order to betray Jesus to them. (Mark 14)

Reflection   Love is faithful, as spring follows winter and as blossoms return to the rose bush. Love is faithful, as the river waters the land and as the tides keep time with the heavens. Love is faithful, as the hen protects her chicks and the moon patrols the night. Love is faithful, as the oak tree withstands the storm and the sun shines in the blizzard. Love is faithful, as a mother hums a lullaby at bedtime, as a father guards the sheepfold against danger. Love is faithful, as the cuckoo fills the summer air and blackberries signal the harvest time. Love is faithful, as the ice-flow yields to rays of sunlight and the one who forgives, forgets. Love is faithful, as the man forgives the boy and the woman embraces the lost child. Love is faithful, as the word of God takes human flesh and signs the promise in blood. Love is faithful, as the invitation to life goes out to all the lands, to every tribe and tongue, to every people and nation. Love is faithful, as God holds the universe in tender hands and fills the human heart with goodness. Love is faithful, because God is faithful and God is love.

The Second Lenten Mystery

Intercessions You are the Faithful Friend.

You led your people out of Egypt and you stayed with them:
You are …
You made a covenant with Abraham and you took your place
beside us: *You are …*
You carved us on the palm of your hand with a love beyond
all telling: *You are …*
You gave us Jesus, our Saviour and our friend, the dawn from
on high: *You are …*
You revealed in Jesus your abundance, your compassion and
your love: *You are …*
You held the candle for us when we betrayed our own
goodness: *You are …*
You led us to life-giving streams when we desired poisoned
cups: *You are …*
You asked us to leave the things that moths destroy and to dig
for treasure: *You are …*
You rolled back the stone of the grave and death was defeated
forever: *You are …*
You sent your Holy Spirit to fill the earth with wisdom and
with truth: *You are …*
You stay with us, in the colours of the skyline, in the strength
of the mountains, in the vastness of the oceans, in the stillness
of the Eucharist: *You are …*

Concluding Prayer God of our highways and God of our
laneways, you are there at the crossroads and you are there on
the mountain face. You gave us Jesus, the Faithful Friend, and
his heart beats in tireless love for us. Our trust is in your
faithfulness and we know that you will be there for our
homecoming. In Jesus Christ we praise your name. Amen.

Jesus is Judged

Opening Prayer We are aware today that an innocent person is about to be judged by the standards of power. Lord, help us to look critically at the systems that we support. With lighted candle we keep watch as the judgement of Rome is given.

Word of God Pilate spoke to them a third time: 'What evil has he done? I find no cause of death in him. I will have him whipped and set him free.' But they kept shouting for Jesus to be crucified and Pilate passed the sentence that they demanded. He set free Barabbas and he handed Jesus over for them to do with him as they wished. (Matthew 27:23-26)

Reflection The power of popular opinion frightens us and the forward march of the fanatic minority is as oppressive today as it was in the first century. In this judgement scene the worst of human nature shows its face and mindless prejudice dictates a death sentence on goodness. As the roar of the mob shouts profanities on our behalf, we see how easily intellects shut down and how quickly we begin to embrace the popular press. As the lust of power and the purity of truth come face to face we must take sides.

Jesus is judged. He bows his head and lets go to love. His love is not an oppressive hand; it is a compassionate heart. It does not protect tomorrow's glory; it is the bread for today. His love is not a filling-up of golden cups; it is an emptying of earthenware vessels. He does not conquer boundaries; he crosses bridges and melts icebergs. The love that defeated Rome is not a tidal wave; it is an ocean breeze. Love remakes;

it is always beginning again. Love renews; it breathes life into dead matter. Love respects; it lets Caesar have his hour. Love reunites; it opens locked doors with rusty keys. Love returns; it swims the deepest oceans and scales the highest peaks. Love remembers; it marks time and keeps holy. Love restores; it forgives seventy-seven times. Love lasts; it rebuilds the road and opens a window in the prison cell. Love lasts; it is timeless in waiting, in hoping, in enduring. Love survives the judgement of the guilty.

The Third Lenten Mystery

Intercessions   May love be our way.

When we gather as Church to remember and to worship: *May love …*
When we gather as family to give and to receive: *May love …*
When we gather as parish to listen and to plan: *May love …*
When we gather as club to celebrate and to participate: *May love …*
When we gather as team to train and to compete: *May love …*
When we gather as staff to work and to relax: *May love …*
When we gather as party to sing and to dance: *May love …*
When we gather as band to laugh and to entertain: *May love …*
When we gather as mourners to weep and to let go: *May love …*

Concluding Prayer   O God, your name is Love. We embrace your call to be a loving presence with you on the soil of the earth. May the love you poured out on us through the heart of Jesus flow in every human system until wars are over and the peace is won. We make our prayer in the name of Jesus Christ who changed all laws into love. Amen.

Jesus is Helped

Opening Prayer   Simon is helping for all of us. We want to be there, to be drawn into the mystery. Lord, as we bring light to this candle, may we carry it for all people who feel the weight of the cross too heavy to bear.

Word of God   On the way they met a man, Simon, and the soldiers forced him to carry Jesus' cross. Simon was from Cyrene and was the father of Alexander and Rufus. (Mark 15)

Reflection   This is my body, walking by the lake, gathering the fish, filling the boat.
This is my body, calling Peter and Andrew, Martha and Mary, asking everything.
This is my body, drawing hearts, needing Simon, knocking on doors, opening locks.
This is my body, finding Zacchaeus, waiting in the night for Nicodemus.
This is my body, healing with a touch, waiting at the deathbed, opening the grave.
This is my body, scanning the distance, lighting a vigil candle for your return.
This is my body, giving up its blood to carry the pain of my people.
This is my body, asking for help to complete a Godly mission.
This is my body, opening the tomb, pushing back the stone of death.
This is my body, rising from the silent grave, splendid as the noonday sun.
This is my body, an eternal flame, spreading fire over the land.

This is my body, leading the dance, bringing the universe to flower.

This is my body, giving in joy, dying with love, holding the web of life.

This is my body, feeding hungry people from age to age.

The Fourth Lenten Mystery

Intercessions   Help us to carry the cross.

In our poverty and in our riches we cry to you: *Help us …*
In our hunger and in our thirst we cry to you: *Help us …*
In our hoping and in our longing we cry to you: *Help us …*
In our want and in our plenty we cry to you: *Help us …*
In our togetherness and in our loneliness we cry to you: *Help us …*
In our fullness and in our emptiness we cry to you: *Help us …*
In our sorrow and in our song we cry to you: *Help us …*
In our despair and in our hope we cry to you: *Help us …*
In our successes and in our failures we cry to you: *Help us …*
In our searching and in our finding we cry to you: *Help us …*
In our dying and in our rising we cry to you: *Help us …*

Concluding Prayer   As a deer longs for water, so our souls long for you, O God. As we make our way back to you, sustain us and ease our burden. Be with us when the cross brings us to the ground. We make our prayer in the name of Jesus, who fell under the weight of the wood. Amen.

Jesus is Recognised

Opening Prayer   Today we are with the people who have followed Jesus, hoping for life, longing for food. We have been drawn into the hope of his teaching and we have come to be near him. The lighted candle speaks to us of a love abundant and for ever.

Word of God   'Our sentence is right because we are getting what we deserve; but he has done no wrong.' And he said to Jesus, 'Remember me, Jesus, when you come as King!' Jesus said to him, 'I promise you that today you will be in paradise with me.' (Luke 23)

Reflection   Your name is Jesus. You will be a saving presence on the earth. Beside you I shall be safe. By day you will walk beside me and by night you will watch as I sleep. You come from a line of kings and you save your people with a law called love.

Your name is Holy and everything you touch turns to fire.
Your name is Holy and everywhere you walk is sacred ground.
Your name is Life and everyone who touches you is transformed.
Your name is Son and those who speak in your name share your family tree.
Your name is Friend and you call me by my name.
Your name is Teacher, the Way, the Truth and the Life.
Your name is Preacher, the one who speaks for God.
Your name is Healer; you take away our fear.
Your name is Pilgrim; you crossed the bridge to life.
Your name is Victory; you broke the chain of sin and death.

Your name is Love; you gave your Body and your Blood.
Your name is Eucharist, the Bread of Life, the Gift Eternal.
Your name is God, yesterday, today and forever.

The Fifth Lenten Mystery

Intercessions   Lord, help us to recognise you.

O God, we stand in a world where human dignity is often denied. May all our decisions call people to life: *Lord, ...*
O God, we live in a world of want and waste, where children go hungry. May we recognise you in your suffering people: *Lord, ...*
O God, we see that the values of greed and ambition threaten all our relationships. May our values be inspired by generosity and the common good: *Lord, ...*
O God, the nations of the world are often entangled in conflicts and wars. May we be people of peace in our time: *Lord, ...*
O God, we witness the suffering of innocent people all of the time. May our voices be loud and clear in defence of justice: *Lord, ...*
O God, many people live in the darkness of despair. May we bring news of the resurrection with us wherever we go: *Lord, ...*

Concluding Prayer   God of our deepest longing, as we gather at your table may we be filled with thanksgiving and joy, for your word is faithful as the dawn. We make our prayer in the name of Jesus who reveals your heart and in the name of the Holy Spirit who breathes your life into all creation. Amen.